CORNING®

W9-BQX-663

AN
AUTUMN
HARVEST OF GOODNESS

CONTENTS

HOME COLLECTION MAISON

Caramelized Onion Crostini

Crostini is a fancy name for toast, but toast topped with these golden onions bathed in balsamic vinegar surely deserves the grander name!

Makes 4 servings.

3 tbsp	*olive oil*	45 mL
2	*large yellow onions, thinly sliced*	2
¼ cup	*balsamic vinegar*	50 mL
1 tsp	*brown sugar*	5 mL
	salt and pepper, to taste	
½ tsp	*dried rosemary, crumbled*	2 mL
1	*small baguette*	1
1	*garlic clove, halved*	1

1. Heat olive oil in a skillet. Add onions and cook over low heat for 15 minutes. Add vinegar, sugar, salt and pepper and continue to simmer another 15 minutes, or until onions begin to caramelize. Sprinkle in rosemary and remove from heat.
2. Toast slices of French bread, rub with cut garlic and spread with the onions. Serve.

CORNING RECOMMENDS
REVERE® Stainless Steel Copper Clad Bottom 10" Skillet and CORNINGWARE® Casual Elegance White Flora™ 14" Embossed Oval Platter

Mushroom Crescents

Lovely little parcels of mushrooms in a cream sauce, perfect with drinks before dinner.
Makes 32 crescents.

2 ½ tbsp	*butter*	37 mL
2 cups	*mushrooms, finely chopped*	500 mL
½ tsp	*lemon juice*	2 mL
I	*green onion, finely chopped*	I
1 ½ tbsp	*flour*	20 mL
I cup	*half-and-half cream*	250 mL
	salt and pepper, to taste	
2 pkg	*refrigerator crescent dough*	2 pkg
I	*egg yolk*	I
I tbsp	*water*	15 mL

1. Melt butter in a skillet. Add mushrooms, lemon juice and onions and sauté until soft.
2. Push mixture to one side of the pan and add flour to the juices. Add cream, salt and pepper, stirring and drawing in the mushroom mixture; continue stirring until thickened. Refrigerate until cool.
3. Preheat oven to 375°F (190°C).
4. Unroll half the crescent dough from one package. With a lightly floured rolling pin on a lightly floured surface, roll dough into an 8-inch (20-cm) square. Cut into four squares, then cut each square into two triangles. Put I tsp (5 mL) of mushroom filling on each triangle. Roll up from the long edge and curve into a crescent shape. Repeat with remaining half of dough, and then with second package. Put crescents on ungreased baking sheet. Brush with egg yolk mixed with water.
5. Bake 10 minutes, or until golden brown.

Pizza Quesadillas for Grown-ups

This is perfect for the times when the grown-ups put their feet up and need a nibble!
Makes 8 servings.

¼ cup	*sun-dried tomatoes — dry packed*	50 mL
4 cups	*shredded mozzarella cheese*	I L
8	*small flour tortillas*	8
4	*prosciutto slices, chopped*	4
¼ cup	*fresh basil leaves*	50 mL
	crushed red pepper flakes, to taste	

1. Soak sun-dried tomatoes in hot water for 20 minutes. Drain and slice.
2. Sprinkle about half the cheese in equal amounts on half of each tortilla.
   Divide the prosciutto, basil leaves and sun-dried tomatoes evenly on top of the
   cheese. Sprinkle with red pepper flakes. Top with remaining cheese and fold
   each tortilla in half.
3. Heat nonstick skillet over medium heat. Cook tortillas 2 to 3 minutes per side
   or until cheese is bubbly.
4. Cut in half and serve with bowls of sour cream and
   salsa for dipping.

CORNING RECOMMENDS
REVERE® Nonstick 12" Skillet
and CORELLE® IMRESSIONS®
Fresh Cut 12 ¼" Serving Platter with
PYREX® STORAGE PLUS®
Round Bowls with Covers

Devilled Artichoke and Ham Spread

Have lots of this on hand when company comes and it will disappear in no time!
Makes 8–10 servings.

1	can (14 oz/398 mL) artichoke hearts	1
1 cup	finely diced ham	250 mL
¾ cup	grated Parmesan cheese	175 mL
½ cup	mayonnaise	125 mL
¼ cup	diced sweet or dill pickle or sliced olives (optional)	50 mL
1 tbsp	chopped fresh basil or 1 tsp dried	15 mL
1 tsp	Russian-style mustard	5 mL
¼ tsp	Worcestershire sauce	1 mL
¼ cup	bread crumbs	50 mL
¼ cup	grated cheddar cheese	50 mL
2 tbsp	chopped fresh parsley	30 mL

1. Drain artichokes. Chop artichokes finely, either by hand or in food processor.
2. In mixing bowl, combine artichokes, ham, Parmesan cheese, mayonnaise, pickles, basil, mustard and Worcestershire.
3. Spoon into buttered 1 ½-qt (1.5-L) casserole.
4. Combine bread crumbs, cheddar cheese and parsley and sprinkle over artichoke mixture.
5. Bake in preheated 325°F (160°C) oven 30 minutes or until golden and bubbly.
6. Serve hot or lukewarm with crackers and fresh vegetables.

Creamy Pumpkin Soup

A big bowl of this soup with some crusty bread and a salad makes a satisfying meal.
Makes 4–6 servings.

¼ cup	*butter*	50 mL
½ cup	*onion*	125 mL
¼ cup	*shallots, chopped*	50 mL
3 cups	*chicken stock, canned or homemade*	750 mL
I	*large potato, peeled and chopped*	I
2 cups	*cooked pumpkin, canned or homemade*	500 mL
I tsp	*paprika*	5 mL
¼ tsp	*crushed red pepper flakes*	I mL
	salt and pepper, to taste	
I cup	*whipping cream*	250 mL
I tbsp	*chopped chives*	15 mL

1. Melt butter in a Dutch oven or large stockpot. Add onion and shallots and sauté for 5 minutes or until soft. Add stock, potato, pumpkin, paprika, red pepper flakes, salt and pepper. Bring to a simmer and cook for 20 minutes, stirring occasionally. Cool slightly then purée in a food processor or blender.
2. Return to pot and stir in most of the cream. Simmer for 5 minutes. Pour into bowls and garnish with a swirl of cream and chives.

CORNING RECOMMENDS
PYREX® Originals™ I-cup Measuring Cup, VISIONS® 5-qt Dutch Oven and CORELLE® IMRESSIONS® Fresh Cut Soup Bowls

Quick South of the Border Pizza

This classic combination of corn, salsa, black beans and cheese makes a welcome change from the usual pizza ingredients.

Makes 4 servings.

4–6	large flour tortillas	4–6
1	recipe, Too Easy Corn, Mexican Style	1
1	can (19 oz/549 mL) black beans, drained and rinsed	1
½	sweet onion, such as Spanish or Vidalia, finely chopped	½
2 cups	shredded Monterey Jack cheese	500 mL
½ cup	pickled jalapeño pepper slices, drained	125 mL
2	large red peppers, roasted and cut in strips	2

1. Preheat oven to 400°F (200°C). Place tortillas on oven rack and cook 3 to 4 minutes, or until crispy and lightly browned.
2. Remove tortillas from oven, place on large baking sheet and spread Too Easy Corn, Mexican Style over tortillas. Sprinkle black beans over, then onion and cheese. Arrange jalapeños and red pepper strips in a spoke-like fashion on top.
3. Bake for 6 to 8 minutes, or until cheese is melted.

Too Easy Corn, Mexican Style

Makes 4 servings.

2 cups	frozen corn niblets	500 mL
½ cup	salsa (homemade or store bought)	125 mL

1. Cook corn according to package directions. When cooked, drain in a colander. Return to saucepan.
2. Stir in salsa, mix thoroughly and warm over low heat for 2 minutes or until heated through. Serve.

CORNING RECOMMENDS
VISIONS® 1 ½-qt Covered Saucepan
and CORELLE® IMRESSIONS®
Enhancements Dinner Plate

Spicy Flank Steak with Lentil Salsa

Flank steak is a very flavourful cut of meat. Make sure you marinate it well and then slice it in thin strips for serving. You'll enjoy every bite!
Makes 4 servings.

Lentil Salsa

½ lb	lentils, cooked and drained*	250 g
½	red onion, diced	½
½	cucumber, seeded and diced	½
2	tomatoes, seeded and chopped	2
2	green onions, chopped	2
1	tin (4 oz/112 g) mild green chili peppers	1
1	jalapeño pepper, seeded and diced (optional)	1
⅓ cup	olive oil	75 mL
¼ cup	red wine vinegar	50 mL
	salt and pepper, to taste	
½ cup	chopped fresh coriander	125 mL
	shredded lettuce, for garnish	

* To cook lentils, rinse and cook, uncovered, in large amount of boiling salted water, until just tender (not mushy), about 45 to 60 minutes. Drain and reserve.

¼ cup	Dijon mustard	50 mL
2 tbsp	honey	30 mL
2 tbsp	molasses	30 mL
2	garlic cloves, minced	2
1 tbsp	vinegar	15 mL
¼ tsp	Tabasco sauce	1 mL
1 lb	flank steak, or other cut of steak	500 g

1. Combine mustard, honey, molasses, garlic, vinegar and Tabasco. Rub mixture into flank steak. Refrigerate overnight.
2. To prepare salsa, combine lentils, onion, cucumber, tomatoes, green onions, green chilis and jalapeño. Whisk together oil, vinegar, salt and pepper. Stir into lentil mixture with coriander. Refrigerate several hours so flavours can blend. Adjust seasoning if necessary. At serving time, spoon over bed of lettuce.
3. To cook steak, preheat broiler and broil approximately 3 minutes per side for medium-rare. Let rest 10 to 15 minutes in warm oven before carving.
4. To serve, slice steak diagonally across grain in thin slices. Serve on top of lentil salsa.

Pasta with Roasted Vegetables

You can adjust the vegetables in this dish to your taste. If you do, make sure there are enough different vegetables to still provide a richness of taste and colour.
Makes 4 servings.

1	large red onion	1
2	small zucchini	2
4	plum tomatoes	4
20	mushrooms, cut in half	20
2	small eggplants	2
1	red pepper	1
1	yellow pepper	1
1	green pepper	1
¼ cup	olive oil	50 mL
1 tbsp	balsamic vinegar	15 mL
½ tsp	dried basil	2 mL
1 tsp	dried oregano	5 mL
2	garlic cloves, chopped	2
	salt and pepper, to taste	
1 lb	pasta (fusilli, rotini or penne)	500 g
2 tbsp	grated Parmesan cheese	30 mL
2 tbsp	flat-leaf Italian parsley	30 mL
¼ tsp	red pepper flakes (optional)	1 mL

1. Cut all vegetables into 1-inch (2.5-cm) chunks. Combine oil, vinegar, basil, oregano, garlic, salt and pepper. Pour over vegetables and toss to coat. Spread vegetables in a roasting dish in a single layer, if possible. Bake for 30 minutes in a preheated 425°F (225°C) oven. Vegetables should be slightly crispy when done.
2. Meanwhile, cook pasta according to package directions then drain. Put into a serving bowl and toss with vegetables and Parmesan cheese. Sprinkle with parsley and red pepper flakes.

Saucy Pasta with Roasted Vegetables

Heat a jar of your favourite tomato sauce and add 1 ½ cups (375 mL) to the Pasta with Roasted Vegetables.

Chili with a Twist

Cocoa in chili: you must be kidding! No kidding — try this and you'll never go back to your old chili ever again.

Makes 6 servings.

4	*hot or sweet Italian sausages*	4
1 ½ lb	*lean ground beef*	750 g
2 tbsp	*olive oil*	30 mL
3	*onions, chopped*	3
6	*garlic cloves, mashed*	6
3	*fresh jalapeño peppers, seeded and chopped, or* *2 tbsp (30 mL) pickled jalapeños, drained and chopped*	3
2 tsp	*salt*	10 mL
1 tbsp	*ground cumin*	15 mL
4 tbsp	*chili powder*	60 mL
1 tbsp	*dried oregano*	15 mL
1	*can (28 oz/796 mL) tomatoes, mashed with juice*	1
½ cup	*salsa*	125 mL
2 tbsp	*cocoa*	30 mL
1	*can (28 oz/796 mL) red kidney beans, drained*	1

Put One Away

Double the recipe, put half in a casserole dish and freeze until needed. Thaw in refrigerator and bake at 350°F (180°C) for 30 to 40 minutes, or until heated through.

CORNING RECOMMENDS
PYREX® STORAGE PLUS®
4-cup Round Bowl and
PYREX® Originals™ 2-qt Casserole

1. Slice sausages into about 6 pieces each, place in 6-qt (6-L) stockpot or Dutch oven and sauté until well browned. Remove to a mixing bowl.
2. Add ground beef to pot and brown. Remove to mixing bowl.
3. Drain fat from pot and add olive oil. Add onions and cook over medium-low heat until they are translucent. Add garlic and cook another minute or two, or until the garlic is fragrant.
4. Return sausage and ground meat to pot. Add jalapeños, salt, cumin, chili powder, oregano, tomatoes, salsa and cocoa. Cover and simmer for 2 hours.
5. Adjust seasoning to taste. Add kidney beans, cover again and cook 30 minutes.

Cod with Tomatoes, Capers and Olives

This combination of fish with tomatoes is reminiscent of Spanish or Portuguese cooking. It's a delicious recipe served with rice on the side.

Makes 6 servings.

2 tbsp	olive oil	30 mL
2	onions, diced	2
2	garlic cloves, chopped	2
	pinch of hot red pepper flakes	
1	can (28 oz / 796 mL) plum tomatoes, broken up	1
1 tsp	dried oregano	5 mL
¼ cup	coarsely chopped black olives	50 mL
2 tbsp	capers, drained	30 mL
	salt and pepper	
6	cod fillets or other fish and shellfish, such as halibut, turbot, sea bass, snapper, shrimp or scallops	6
2 tbsp	chopped parsley	30 mL

1. Heat oil in a large saucepan. Add onions, garlic and pepper flakes and cook until onions are softened, about 5 minutes.
2. Add tomatoes and oregano and cook over medium-high heat until sauce has thickened slightly, about 10 minutes. Stir in olives and capers and season with salt and pepper.
3. Spoon half the sauce into a lightly oiled shallow casserole dish. Arrange fish over sauce. Spoon remaining sauce over fish.
4. Bake at 375°F (190°C) for 10 minutes or until fish is just cooked through. Sprinkle with parsley before serving.

Pork and Apple Sauté

Pork and apples together are a classic taste combination, and this recipe is a wonderful way to try these flavours if you haven't already.
Makes 6 servings.

¼ cup	olive oil	50 mL
3	firm apples, peeled, cored and sliced	3
2	pork tenderloins, trimmed of fat	2
½ cup	flour, seasoned with salt and pepper	125 mL
1 cup	apple cider	250 mL
¼ cup	lemon juice	50 mL
½ tsp	dried rosemary or thyme	2 mL
	salt and pepper, to taste	
2 tbsp	chopped parsley	30 mL

1. Heat 2 tbsp (30 mL) olive oil in large skillet. Add apple slices and cook over medium heat until tender and starting to caramelize, about 10 minutes. Remove and keep warm.
2. While apples are cooking, cut tenderloin at an angle into ⅓-inch (8-mm) cutlets. Pound thin using meat mallet or pounder.
3. Heat remaining oil in same skillet. Dust cutlets with flour, then cook in two batches over medium-high heat, browning on each side. Remove to serving dish. Arrange apple slices over pork. Keep warm.
4. Return pan to heat. Add apple cider, lemon juice and rosemary. Bring to boil and cook about 4 to 5 minutes to reduce sauce slightly. Season with salt and pepper.
5. Pour sauce over pork. Garnish with parsley.

Tasty Barbecued Chicken with Corncakes

A great quick chicken dish to put together at the end of a work day, even if the corncakes have to wait for another day.

Makes 6 servings.

2	*jalapeño peppers*	2
I	*small onion, cut into wedges*	I
I	*garlic clove*	I
½ cup	*apricot jam*	125 mL
½ cup	*tomato sauce*	125 mL
2 tbsp	*red wine vinegar*	30 mL
I tbsp	*Worcestershire sauce*	15 mL
I tbsp	*Dijon mustard*	15 mL
6	*single, boneless, skinless chicken breasts*	6

1. Combine peppers, onion and garlic in bowl of food processor and chop fine. Add jam, tomato sauce, vinegar, Worcestershire and mustard and blend until smooth.
2. Pour sauce over chicken breasts. Cover and marinate 3 to 4 hours in refrigerator.
3. Preheat barbecue to medium-high. Brush grill with oil. Place chicken on grill and cook 5 minutes per side or until cooked through. Or bake in a preheated 400°F (200°C) oven for 30 minutes. Serve with corncakes.
4. For corncakes, combine flour, cornmeal, baking powder, baking soda, salt and pepper. Stir together corn kernels, buttermilk and butter. Add to dry ingredients.
5. Heat large nonstick griddle pan or skillet and brush with oil. Pour about ⅓ cup (75 mL) batter in pan and cook over medium heat until bubbles appear on top. Turn and cook other side. Keep warm in low oven. Repeat using remaining batter. Corncakes can be cooked earlier and refrigerated, then brushed lightly with oil and reheated on barbecue.

Corncakes

Makes 6 servings.

¾ cup	*all-purpose flour*	175 mL
½ cup	*cornmeal*	125 mL
I ½ tsp	*baking powder*	7 mL
½ tsp	*baking soda*	2 mL
½ tsp	*salt*	2 mL
¼ tsp	*freshly ground black pepper*	I mL
I ¼ cups	*fresh corn kernels (about 2 cobs)*	300 mL
I ½ cups	*buttermilk*	375 mL
2 tbsp	*melted butter*	30 mL
2 tbsp	*vegetable oil*	30 mL

Tuna Melt Bagels

These bagels make a great quick dinner, and if you're really pressed for time, you can simply leave out some of the ingredients other than the basics — the tuna, bagels, mayo, onions and cheese.

Makes 2 servings.

I	*can (7 oz/198 g) chunk tuna, drained and flaked*	I
⅓ cup	*mayonnaise*	75 mL
⅓ cup	*sun-dried tomato pesto*	75 mL
½ cup	*diced celery*	125 mL
2	*green onions, chopped*	2
¼ cup	*chopped dill pickle*	50 mL
2 tbsp	*chopped parsley*	30 mL
	salt and pepper, to taste	
2	*bagels, cut in half crosswise*	2
¼ cup	*grated Parmesan cheese*	50 mL

1. In a bowl, combine tuna, mayonnaise, pesto, celery, onions, pickle, parsley and salt and pepper. Mix thoroughly.
2. Place bagel halves on a baking sheet. Bake in preheated 375°F (190°C) oven for 10 minutes, or until lightly browned. Spread tuna mixture over bagels. Sprinkle with Parmesan cheese.
3. Return to oven for another 8 minutes, or until heated through and top is golden. Serve hot.

Sweet and Sour Beef Stir-fry

Stir-fry dishes are popular because they're quick and tasty. Try this one!
Makes 4 servings.

¾ lb	*beef (flank steak, sirloin, etc.), thinly sliced*	375 g
1 tbsp	*soya sauce*	15 mL
1 tbsp	*rice wine*	15 mL
1 tbsp	*cornstarch*	15 mL
1 cup	*beef stock or chicken stock or water*	250 mL
⅓ cup	*ketchup*	75 mL
¼ cup	*brown sugar*	50 mL
3 tbsp	*rice or white vinegar*	45 mL
2 tbsp	*soya sauce*	30 mL
1 tsp	*sesame oil*	5 mL
½ tsp	*hot chili paste*	2 mL
1 tbsp	*cornstarch*	15 mL
2 tbsp	*vegetable oil*	30 mL
1 tbsp	*chopped fresh ginger root*	15 mL
2	*garlic cloves, chopped*	2
3	*green onions, chopped*	3
¾ lb	*green beans, cut in 2-inch (5-cm) lengths*	375 g
1	*red pepper, cut in strips*	1

1. Combine beef with soya sauce, wine and cornstarch. Marinate 30 to 60 minutes.
2. Combine stock, ketchup, sugar, vinegar, soya sauce, sesame oil, chili paste and cornstarch and stir well. Reserve.
3. To cook, heat oil in nonstick wok. Add beef and stir-fry until pinkness just disappears. Remove from wok. Add ginger, garlic and onions. Stir-fry for 30 seconds. Add beans and pepper and cook for 3 minutes. Stir sauce. Add to wok and cook until mixture boils and thickens slightly, and vegetables are just tender.
4. Stir in beef and toss well to combine.

Lasagna Rolls

A slightly new take on lasagna, yet still safe enough for those who prefer the traditional!
Makes 5 servings.

2 tbsp	olive oil	30 mL
1	small onion, chopped	1
2	garlic cloves, minced	2
1	can (28 oz / 796 mL) plum tomatoes	1
1 tsp	oregano	5 mL
1 tsp	basil	5 mL
	pinch of sugar	
	salt and pepper, to taste	
10	lasagna noodles	10
1 cup	ricotta cheese	250 mL
1 cup	Parmesan cheese	250 mL
1 ½ cups	shredded mozzarella cheese	375 mL
1 cup	cooked spinach (or defrosted frozen, squeezed dry)	250 mL
2	eggs	2
	salt and pepper, to taste	

Put One Away

Double the recipe and freeze one dish for future use. Thaw overnight in refrigerator, then bake at 350°F (180°C) for 25 minutes or until thoroughly baked.

CORNING RECOMMENDS

PYREX® Originals™ 1-pt Measuring Cup and CORNINGWARE® FRENCH WHITE® 2 ½-qt Covered Oval Casserole

1. To make tomato sauce, heat oil in saucepan, add onion and garlic and sauté 5 minutes. Add tomatoes, oregano, basil, sugar and salt and pepper and simmer covered for 30 minutes, stirring occasionally. Put sauce in a food processor and mix for 30 seconds. Put 1 cup (250 mL) into a casserole dish.
2. Cook noodles in boiling salted water until al dente, about 10 minutes. Drain and pat dry. Mix together ricotta, Parmesan, 1 cup (250 mL) mozzarella, spinach, eggs and salt and pepper.
3. Spread about 3 tbsp (45 mL) of the mixture on one side of each noodle. Roll up the noodles and place them on their ends in the casserole dish, on top of the sauce. Make sure the noodles stand upright. Pour remaining tomato sauce over noodles and sprinkle with remaining mozzarella cheese. Bake in a preheated 350°F (180°C) oven for 25 minutes.

Chicken Strip Tacos

This is a great dish to introduce Mexican flavours to the reluctant eater!
Makes 4 servings.

4	*single, boneless, skinless chicken breasts*	4
1 tbsp	*olive oil*	15 mL
2	*garlic cloves, minced*	2
1	*small onion, sliced*	1
1 tsp	*chili powder*	5 mL
½ tsp	*cumin*	2 mL
¼ tsp	*oregano*	1 mL
	salt and pepper, to taste	
	Tabasco sauce, to taste	
8	*taco shells*	8
1 ½ cups	*lettuce, shredded*	375 mL
1 cup	*salsa, homemade or store bought*	250 mL
1 cup	*shredded cheddar cheese*	250 mL

1. Cut each chicken breast in half crosswise, then slice into thin strips.
2. Heat oil in a skillet over medium heat. Add garlic and onion and sauté about 3 minutes. Add chicken, chili powder, cumin, oregano, salt and pepper and stir frequently until golden brown, about 6 minutes. Sprinkle on Tabasco, to taste.
3. Put taco shells in a glass pie plate and microwave for 30 seconds or warm in a 350°F (180°C) oven for 10 minutes.
4. To serve, put chicken in shells and top with lettuce, salsa and cheese.

Spicy Baked Beans

This is a tangy version of baked beans that you'll want to make over and over again!
Makes 6 servings.

2 cups	*dried navy beans*	500 mL
½ lb	*bacon*	250 g
I	*large onion, sliced*	I
¼ cup	*brown sugar*	50 mL
3 tbsp	*molasses*	45 mL
I tsp	*salt*	5 mL
¼ tsp	*dry mustard*	I mL
¼ tsp	*pepper*	I mL
⅓ cup	*extra spicy barbecue sauce*	75 mL

1. Soak beans overnight in 6 cups (I ½ L) of cold water. Drain and rinse. Place in a 3-qt saucepan with 6 cups (I ½ L) of fresh cold water. Bring to a boil and simmer uncovered 45 minutes, or until tender. Drain beans, reserving liquid.

2. Heat oven to 300°F (150°C). Cut bacon slices into thirds. Put a layer of onion and bacon slices in an ungreased 2 ½-qt casserole. Add half the beans, another layer of bacon and onion, the remaining beans, and end with a top layer of bacon and onion.

3. Stir together sugar, molasses, salt, dry mustard and pepper and I cup (250 mL) of reserved liquid. Pour over beans and add enough of the remaining liquid or water to cover the beans.

4. Cover and bake for 2 hours. Remove cover and stir in barbecue sauce. Bake uncovered for I ½ hours, stirring occasionally.

Cornish Hens with Rice Stuffing and Spiced Glaze

All you need with this dish is some buttered baby carrots and a tossed salad and you've got an impressive dinner to serve family or friends.

Makes 6–8 servings.

Rice Stuffing

3 cups	chicken broth (canned or homemade)	750 mL
1 ½ cups	uncooked converted rice	375 mL
½	onion, finely diced	½
2	celery stalks, finely diced	2
1	red pepper, finely diced	1
3 oz	pecan halves or pieces, toasted, then chopped	75 g
⅓ cup	butter, melted	75 mL
2 tbsp	minced fresh parsley	30 mL
1 tsp	dried thyme	5 mL
1 tsp	dried mustard	5 mL
	salt and pepper	

CORNING RECOMMENDS

PYREX® Originals™ 1-cup Measuring Cup and PYREX® Originals™ BAKE 'N' SERVE Set with 3-qt Oblong Baking Dish and Brown Rattan Basket

4	Cornish hens	4
½ cup	apple jelly	125 mL
½ cup	chicken broth	125 mL
½ tsp	allspice	2 mL
½ tsp	ground cinnamon	2 mL

1. To make stuffing, bring 3 cups (750 mL) of the chicken broth to a boil, stir in rice then reduce heat. When rice is cooked, put in a bowl and add onion, celery, red pepper, pecans, butter, parsley, thyme, mustard and salt and pepper. Mix well.
2. Preheat oven to 375°F (190°C). Clean hens and, using large cleaver, cut each hen through breastbone to form two halves.
3. In a well-greased 3-qt (3-L) baking dish, form 8 mounds of rice stuffing and position half a hen, cavity side down, on each. Sprinkle with salt and pepper. Put in oven.
4. In a small saucepan, heat apple jelly, ½ cup (125 mL) chicken broth, allspice and cinnamon until jelly is melted.
5. After hens have cooked for 20 minutes, spoon some glaze over them and then return to oven. Baste with glaze again after another 20 minutes.
6. Continue to bake until hens are thoroughly cooked. Serve.

Hearty Mexican Pork Stew

This is a delicious alternative to beef stew, a really flavourful dish to warm you up when the chill winds of autumn blow.

Makes 4 servings.

2 tbsp	olive oil	30 mL
2 lb	boneless, lean pork, cut in 1-inch (2.5-cm) cubes	1 kg
	salt and pepper, to taste	
1	large onion, diced	1
2	large garlic cloves, pressed	2
2	cans (28 oz/796 mL) tomatoes, mashed	
½ cup	tomato salsa	125 mL
3 tbsp	minced jalapeño peppers, fresh or pickled	45 mL
¼ cup	minced fresh parsley	50 mL
2 tsp	ground cumin	10 mL
1 tsp	oregano	5 mL
1 tsp	dried thyme	5 mL
¼ tsp	crushed red pepper	1 mL
2 cups	chicken stock (canned or homemade)	500 mL
5	large potatoes, peeled and diced	5
	sour cream, to garnish	

1. Heat oil in 6-qt (6 L) stockpot and brown meat. Remove meat from pot and season with salt and pepper, to taste.
2. Add more oil to the pot, if necessary, then sauté onion and garlic until onions are translucent.
3. Add tomatoes, salsa, jalapeños, parsley, cumin, oregano, thyme, crushed red pepper and chicken stock. Bring to a boil, cover and reduce heat. Simmer for 2 hours. Adjust seasonings if necessary.
4. Add potatoes and simmer until potatoes are cooked through, about 30 minutes.
5. Serve in bowls with a dollop of sour cream on top.

CORNING RECOMMENDS

REVERE® Stainless Steel Aluminum Disc Bottom 6-qt Stockpot with CORELLE® IMRESSIONS® Callaway Soup Bowl

Wild Rice with Apricots and Pistachios

The delicious taste of wild rice has such a robust flavour that it is best served with something quite simple like roasted chicken.

Makes 4 servings.

2 tbsp	*butter*	30 mL
I	*onion, finely chopped*	I
2	*garlic cloves, chopped*	2
I ½ cups	*wild rice*	375 mL
½ cup	*diced dried apricots*	125 mL
½ cup	*chopped pistachios*	125 mL
½ tsp	*thyme*	2 mL
3 ½ cups	*chicken stock, homemade or canned*	825 mL
	salt and pepper, to taste	
2 tbsp	*chopped parsley*	30 mL

1. Melt butter in a large saucepan. Cook onion and garlic until soft.
2. Stir in rice, apricots and pistachios. Stir to coat with butter. Add thyme, chicken stock, salt and pepper.
3. Cover and bring to a boil. Reduce heat and cook 50 to 60 minutes or until rice is tender. Add extra stock if rice is dry. Alternatively, if liquid remains, remove cover and cook to evaporate liquid.
4. Adjust seasoning. Stir in parsley.

CORNING RECOMMENDS
VISIONS® 2 ½-qt Covered Saucepan and Sculptured PYREX® 4 ½-qt Salad Bowl with Dark Blue Plastic Storage Cover

Curried Onions and Potatoes

Try this with hamburgers or fish for a change from French fries. The curry flavour is very subtle and the taste is delicious!

Makes 4 servings.

2 tbsp	*water*	30 mL
2 tbsp	*butter*	30 mL
1 tbsp	*curry powder*	15 mL
1	*garlic clove, minced*	1
	pepper, to taste	
2	*large onions, cut into wedges*	2
4	*large potatoes, peeled and cut into chunks*	4
½ cup	*sour cream or yogurt*	125 mL

1. Preheat oven to 350°F (180°C). Measure water, butter, curry powder, garlic and pepper into a 4-qt (4-L) baking dish. Put in oven until butter melts.
2. Stir vegetables into curry mixture until each piece is coated with mixture. Cover.
3. Bake until potatoes are tender, about 40 minutes. Stir occasionally during cooking. Remove dish from oven, stir in sour cream and serve.

CORNING RECOMMENDS
CORNINGWARE® CLASSICS™
Summer Blush 4-qt Open Roaster with
Summer Blush Dessert/Salad Plate

Cornmeal Cheddar Bread

This is a delicious side dish to any Mexican-flavoured meal. Remember to freeze one of the loaves to have next time!

Makes 2 loaves.

1 cup	*boiling water*	250 mL
⅓ cup	*cornmeal*	75 mL
½ tsp	*sugar*	2 mL
½ cup	*lukewarm water*	125 mL
1 package	*active dry yeast or 1 tbsp/15 mL*	1
1 ½ cups	*warm water or milk*	375 mL
2 tsp	*salt*	10 mL
2 tbsp	*brown sugar*	30 mL
1 ¼ cups	*grated old cheddar cheese*	300 mL
5 to 5 ½ cups	*unbleached all-purpose flour (or more)*	1.25 to 1.35 L

1. Pour boiling water over cornmeal and let stand until just warm.
2. Stir together sugar and lukewarm water. Sprinkle yeast over top and let stand until doubled in volume.
3. In a large mixing bowl, combine warm water, salt, brown sugar, 1 cup (250 mL) cheddar cheese, cornmeal mixture and yeast mixture. Stir well. Add flour 1 cup (250 mL) at a time. When dough becomes too stiff to stir, turn out onto a floured surface. Knead in additional flour until dough is no longer sticky. Knead dough 10 minutes.
4. Place dough in a lightly oiled bowl. Cover with plastic and let rise until doubled in volume, about 1 to 1 ½ hours. Punch dough down and divide in half. Shape into two loaves and place into buttered loaf pans. Let rise again until doubled in volume. Carefully sprinkle remaining cheese over bread.
5. Bake at 375°F (190°C) for 30 to 35 minutes or until golden and sides of loaf are also golden. Remove bread from pans and cool completely on wire racks.

Island Sweet Potatoes

This is "island" style because of its use of ginger, curry and mango chutney. What a tasty way to prepare sweet potatoes!

Makes 6 servings.

1 ½ lb	*sweet potatoes, peeled and cut in to chunks*	750 g
1 ½ lb	*carrots, peeled and cut in to chunks*	750 g
2 tbsp	*butter*	30 mL
1	*small onion, diced*	1
2	*garlic cloves, minced*	2
2 tbsp	*chopped fresh ginger root*	30 mL
½ tsp	*curry powder*	2 mL
½ cup	*mango chutney*	125 mL
	salt and pepper, to taste	

1. Cook potatoes and carrots in boiling water until tender. Drain, reserving some cooking liquid.

2. In a small pan, melt butter. Cook onion, garlic and ginger until soft but not brown. Add curry powder and cook another minute.

3. Purée potatoes and carrots using a food processor or food mill, or mash with a potato masher. Mix in curry mixture and chutney. If mixture is too thick, thin with reserved cooking liquid. Season to taste with salt and pepper. Serve hot.

CORNING RECOMMENDS

VISIONS® 2 ½-qt Covered Saucepan and PYREX® STORAGE PLUS® 3 ½-cup or 6-cup Rectangular Dish with Dark Teal Plastic Storage Cover

Onion and Red Pepper Marmalade with Sage

A lovely accompaniment to roasted meats and poultry.
Makes 6–10 servings.

3 tbsp	*olive oil*	45 mL
3	*medium onions, sliced thinly*	3
3	*garlic cloves, chopped*	3
3	*peppers (red, yellow or a combination of colours), roasted, peeled and thinly sliced*	3
2 tbsp	*chopped fresh sage*	30 mL
½ tsp	*salt*	2 mL
	freshly ground black pepper, to taste	

1. Heat oil in skillet. Add onions and garlic and cook over medium heat until soft and golden, about 15 minutes. Stir frequently and reduce heat as necessary. Spoon into a serving dish.
2. Add peppers and their juices, sage and salt and pepper. Toss well. Serve warm or refrigerate for up to 5 days.

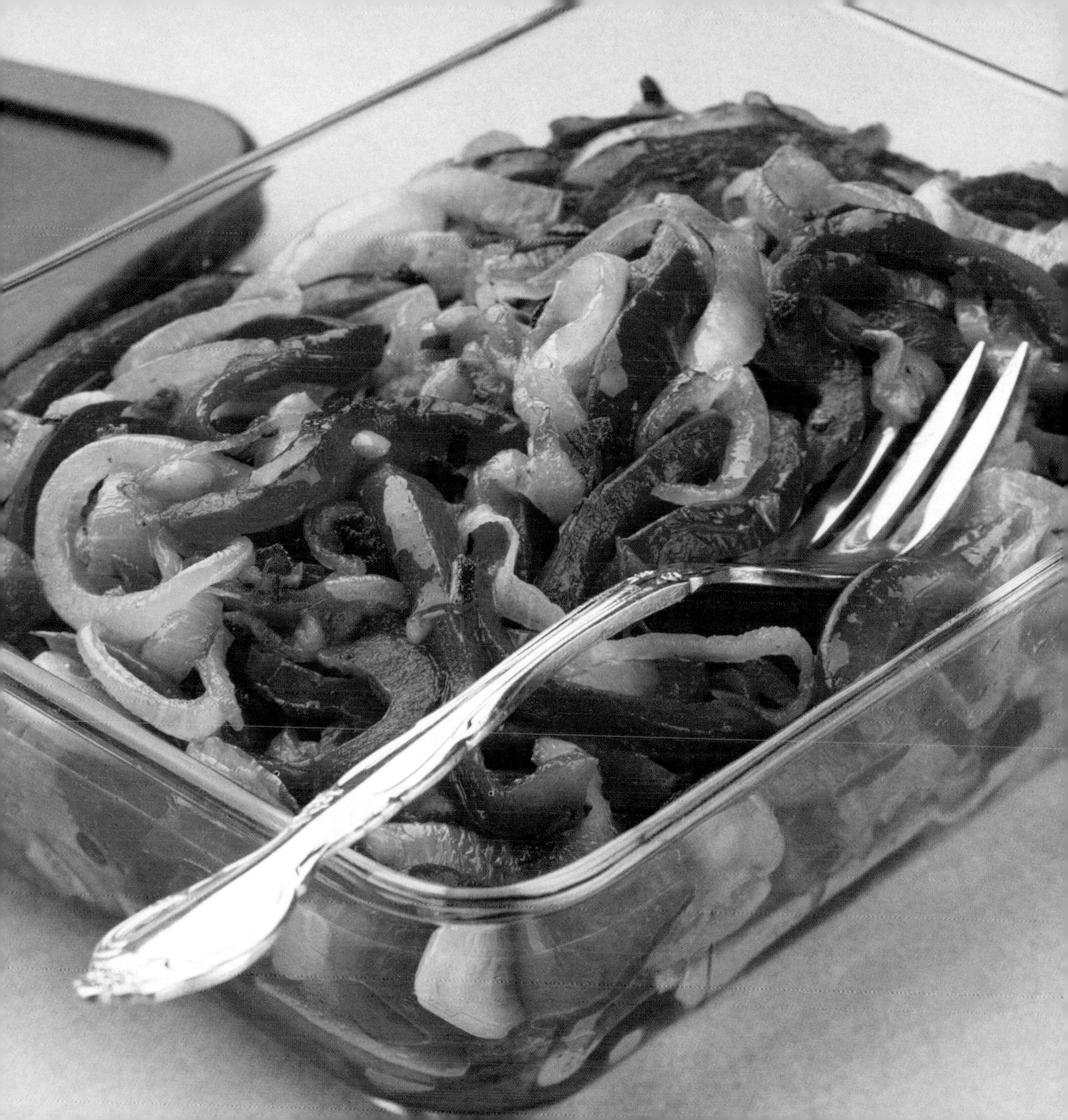

Broccoli Chinese Style

A really tasty and quick way to dress up broccoli. Delicious served with grilled steak or salmon.

Makes 4 servings.

1 lb	broccoli	500 g
3 tbsp	soya sauce	45 mL
4 tbsp	water	60 mL
2 tsp	grated fresh ginger root	10 mL
2	garlic cloves, minced	2
2 tsp	brown sugar	10 mL
1 tbsp	olive oil	15 mL

1. Wash broccoli and slice lengthwise so that the stems are thin.
2. To make sauce, combine soya sauce, water, ginger, garlic and sugar in a bowl. Set aside.
3. Heat oil in a large skillet or wok. Stir-fry broccoli in oil for 3 minutes. Add sauce, stir well, put lid on pan and allow broccoli to steam for 3 to 5 minutes, or until tender.
4. Serve with sauce.

CORNING RECOMMENDS
REVERE® Nonstick
Stir-Fry Polished Aluminum Pan
and CORELLE® IMRESSIONS®
Fresh Cut Serving Platter

Apple Crisp

If ever there was a comfort food, this is it! Warm apple crisp on a cool fall evening — yum!

Makes 4 servings.

4 cups	*peeled and sliced apples*	I L
½ cup	*raisins*	125 mL
¼ cup	*butter*	50 mL
⅔ cup	*brown sugar*	150 mL
½ cup	*oats*	125 mL
½ cup	*flour*	125 mL
I tsp	*cinnamon*	5 mL
½ cup	*chopped walnuts*	125 mL

1. Preheat oven to 375°F (190°C).
2. Put apples and raisins into an 8-inch (20-cm) square pan.
3. To make the topping, melt butter and mix with remaining ingredients. Sprinkle topping evenly over fruit.
4. Bake for 30 to 35 minutes until apples are tender.
5. Serve warm with a little cream or ice cream.

Blueberry Crisp

Substitute 4 cups (I L) blueberries for apples and omit raisins and walnuts.

Ginger Amaretti Peaches

What a combination: peaches and ginger! If you have trouble finding amaretti cookies, another crisp cookie of your choosing can be substituted.

Makes 4 servings.

* To peel peaches, drop in boiling water for 30 seconds. Cool in cold water. Peel.

8	peaches, peeled* and sliced	8
2 tbsp	lemon juice	30 mL
2 tbsp	brown sugar	30 mL
1 cup	crumbled amaretti cookies	250 mL
2 tbsp	chopped candied ginger	30 mL
½ tsp	cinnamon	2 mL
¼ cup	brown sugar	50 mL
2 tbsp	melted butter	30 mL
¾ cup	thick sour cream	175 mL
2 tbsp	orange liqueur or peach brandy	30 mL

1. In a mixing bowl, combine peach slices with lemon juice and brown sugar. Spoon into lightly buttered 8-inch (2-L) baking dish.
2. In another bowl, combine amaretti crumbs, ginger, cinnamon, sugar and butter. Sprinkle topping over peaches.
3. Bake in preheated 350°F (180°C) oven for 25 to 30 minutes until peaches are cooked.
4. Combine sour cream and liqueur. Pass separately or serve alongside peaches.

CORNING RECOMMENDS
PYREX® Originals™ 2 ½-qt Mixing Bowl, PYREX® Originals™ 8" Square Cake Dish with Dark Blue Plastic Storage Cover and CORELLE® IMRESSIONS® Fruit Basket Dinner Plate

Pineapple Blueberry Sundae

Everyone loves a sundae — this one is a treat for guests and family alike!
Makes 4 servings.

2 cups	blueberries, frozen (unthawed)	500 mL
⅔ cup	orange juice	150 mL
4 tbsp	sugar	60 mL
½ tsp	cinnamon	2 mL
1 tbsp	finely grated orange peel	15 mL
4	fresh pineapple slices	4
4	scoops of vanilla ice cream	4

1. Combine blueberries, juice, sugar, cinnamon and orange peel in a saucepan and bring to a boil. Turn down heat and simmer 8 to 10 minutes until sauce has slightly thickened. Remove from heat and cool.
2. Put a pineapple slice in each of four bowls. Top each with a scoop of ice cream and pour the blueberry sauce over top.

Fruity Streusel Cake

This is a very versatile dessert. It is different — yet just as good — every time you change the fruits.

Makes 6 servings.

¾ cup	*butter*	175 mL
¾ cup	*white sugar*	175 mL
I	*egg*	I
2 ½ cups	*flour*	625 mL
4 tsp	*baking powder*	20 mL
½ tsp	*cinnamon*	2 mL
4 cups	*sliced fruit (apples, plums, peaches or blueberries, etc.)*	I L

1. Heat oven to 375°F (190°C).
2. Cream butter, sugar and egg together. Mix flour, baking powder and cinnamon together and add to butter mixture. Batter will be crumbly. Pat three-quarters of the mixture into an 8-inch cake dish.
3. Put sliced fruit on top of mixture. Sprinkle remaining crumbs on top. Bake for 35 to 40 minutes until cake is bubbly and browned.
4. Serve hot with ice cream.

CORNING RECOMMENDS

PYREX® Originals™ I-pt Measuring Cup, PYREX® Originals™ 8" Square Cake Dish and CORELLE® IMRESSIONS® Enhancement Salad/Pasta Bowl

Peach Upside-down Cake

This may seem old-fashioned but it is one of those desserts everyone always loves because nobody makes it!

Makes 8 servings.

⅓ cup	*vegetable shortening*	75 mL
¾ cup	*sugar*	175 mL
1	*egg*	1
1 tsp	*vanilla*	5 mL
1 ¾ cup	*flour*	425 mL
3 tsp	*baking powder*	15 mL
½ tsp	*salt*	2 mL
¾ cup	*milk*	175 mL
3 tbsp	*butter*	45 mL
½ cup	*brown sugar*	125 mL
2	*cans (14 oz/396 mL) peach halves*	2

1. Preheat oven to 350°F (180°C). Cream together shortening, sugar, egg and vanilla. Beat until light and fluffy. Sift together flour, baking powder and salt. Add to creamed mixture with milk and beat for 2 minutes.

2. Melt butter in an 8-inch (20-cm) square pan in the microwave for about 30 seconds. Sprinkle butter with brown sugar. Drain peaches and place a single layer, flat side up, on top of the sugar. Pour cake mixture over the peaches.

3. Bake 35 to 40 minutes until a toothpick inserted in the centre comes out clean. Let cool for 10 minutes, then run a knife around the edge of the cake. Put a serving plate upside down on the cake and flip it over. The peaches will be on top.

Frozen Baked Pie with Orange and Almonds

The flavours in this frozen treat are scrumptious and it's always fun to serve guests ice cream straight from the oven!

Makes 6 servings.

I ½ cups	*graham wafer crumbs*	375 mL
I tsp	*cinnamon*	5 mL
⅓ cup	*melted butter*	75 mL
I cup	*whipping cream*	250 mL
I tsp	*vanilla*	5 mL
¼ cup	*orange liqueur (e.g., Grand Marnier)*	50 mL
⅔ cup	*sugar*	150 mL
I tsp	*grated orange peel*	5 mL
¼ cup	*sliced almonds, toasted*	50 mL
¼ cup	*candied peel*	50 mL
5	*egg whites*	5

Put One Away

Double the recipe and keep one pie frozen until needed. Proceed with baking as per directions given.

1. Mix crumbs, cinnamon and melted butter together and pat into pie plate. Bake at 350°F (180°C) for 10 minutes, then cool.
2. Whip cream until soft peaks form, add vanilla, liqueur and ⅓ cup (75 mL) of sugar. Fold in orange peel, almonds and candied peel.
3. Beat 2 egg whites until stiff and fold into cream. Mound in crust and freeze until completely solid.
4. Preheat oven to 400°F (200°C). Beat 3 egg whites with remaining ⅓ cup (75 mL) sugar until stiff. Spoon over frozen cream and spread right to the edge of the plate.
5. Bake pie until golden, about 5 minutes.

Index

Produced exclusively for Corning Canada Inc., 60 Leek Crescent, Richmond Hill, Ontario Canada L4B 1H1 by Alpha Corporation/Susan Yates, Publisher
Photographs by Peter Paterson/Paterson Photographic Works Inc.
Copy Editor: Wendy Thomas
Editorial Services: Colborne Communications Centre
Text Cover and Design: Dave Murphy/Artplus Ltd.
Page Layout: Valerie Bateman & Leanne Knox/Artplus Ltd.
Printed and bound in Canada by Transcontinental Printing Inc.

For product information call: 905-771-3575

ISBN: 1-896391-24-9

Distributed by Canadian Tire Corporation